You carry within you,
the wonders that you seek.

Let not the storms of the world,
ever make you weak.

Reflections
of a
Wandering Heart

Reflections of a Wandering Heart

A Poetic Journey

Shilpi Goyal

RUPA

Published by
Rupa Publications India Pvt. Ltd 2023
7/16, Ansari Road, Daryaganj
New Delhi 110002

Sales centres:
Bengaluru Chennai Hyderabad
Jaipur Kathmandu Kolkata
Mumbai Prayagraj

Copyright © Shilpi Goyal 2023
Illustration courtesy: Bazma Ahmad

This is a work of fiction. Names, characters, places and incidents are either the product of the author's imagination or are used fictitiously and any resemblance to any actual person, living or dead, events or locales is entirely coincidental.

All rights reserved.
No part of this publication may be reproduced, transmitted, or stored in a retrieval system, in any form or by any means, electronic, mechanical, photocopying, recording or otherwise, without the prior permission of the publisher.

P-ISBN: 978-93-5702-317-7
E-ISBN: 978-93-5702-639-0

First impression 2023

10 9 8 7 6 5 4 3 2 1

The moral right of the author has been asserted.

Printed in India

This book is sold subject to the condition that it shall not, by way of trade or otherwise, be lent, resold, hired out, or otherwise circulated, without the publisher's prior consent, in any form of binding or cover other than that in which it is published.

*Dedicated to all who believe in miracles
and the magic of being alive;
who understand the basic philosophy of life
and live in awe of the wonders around them.*

*Dedicated to all who believe that a soft heart
with a strong mind is the best combination;
and to all wandering hearts who love
and live their journey.*

Contents

Foreword / ix

Preface / xi

The Healer / 2

I Am Like You / 5

The Storm / 8

Magnificent Macabre / 11

The Space Between / 15

Home / 18

Being Good: The Distortion / 20

Pause / 23

Lost Souls / 27

Loner / 31

Young Love / 34

Travel Diary / 36

The Essence of a Woman / 39

Confused / 42

Art / 45

Reminiscence / 47

Draupadi / 50

Taken for Granted / 54

Resonance / 57

Dusk / 59

More or Less / 62

Perfectly Fine / 64

Conviction / 66

Grief / 68

Hourglass / 71

To Where It Belongs / 75

Maa / 78

Love Letter / 81

Abode / 84

My Portable Home / 86

Too Much / 88

Parched / 89

That One Person / 91

Mirage / 93

Is Your Wrong, Right? / 95

2050 / 100

One-Sided Love / 104

Solo Trip / 107

That Love Story / 112

See Yourself / 114

Acknowledgements / 116

Foreword

Shilpi Goyal's *Reflections of a Wandering Heart: A Poetic Journey* is like witnessing the glorious moon when the curtain of clouds covering its countenance is suddenly lifted by a strong wind on a dark night.

Shilpi begins with a frank admission. She confesses that though she had been burdened with inhibitions and self-doubt, she had cast them away with a firm determination to launch out on her own and to be herself without fear!

True to her intention, Shilpi wanders over a wide and varied landscape in her poetic journey. Her poetic canvas dwells upon and includes reflections on being a true woman with no reactionary intention, desire or desperation of proving herself to be equal to men. Her verses refer to facing life with courage, on accepting others and ourselves fully with our strengths as well as our flaws. While on the one hand, she dwells on man's limitless yearnings, on the other, she talks of the merits of forgiveness, of the positive impact of being kind on ourselves as well as others.

Instead of joining the 'rat race' in which humanity seems to be constantly running, her poetry gently cautions its readers to resist the popular urge to keep chasing the worldly glory, perfection and triumphs. Instead of running after shadows, she prompts us to turn our gaze on the value of the seemingly small things in life.

Much of what this poetess writes has universal appeal. For instance, in 'I Am Like You', she talks of how we humans start showing characteristics and qualities that we have inherited or imbibed from our parents, teachers or those we hold in high regard.

But in many of her poems, Shilpi's innate Indianness shines through. This characteristic is evident in her reflections about women in 'The Essence of a Woman'.

Again, a belief in rebirth which is part of ancient Hindu philosophy, seems to show in 'I Am Like You'. In the poem, she stresses how we humans recognize our distinct identity or voice and also feel we are far more old than what our real age might reflect. This seems apparent, for instance, where she writes:

'You've only arrived here couple of decades ago. But you've lived a hundred years, that's what you feel.'

In short, here we have a poetess with a sensitive soul and considerable depth of thought. Other distinct qualities that she possesses are that she writes with sincerity, clarity and simplicity. Though full of humanity and humility, the poetess is never overly apologetic or humble. There is wisdom in much of what she conveys but instead of sounding preachy or harsh, her verses always tend to lift, encourage and produce a positive impact.

Shilpi writes with considerable ease and facility and her language is free from instances that might reveal that English is not her mother tongue.

Due to its subject matter, its qualities of being unpretentious and genuine and the positivity of its impact, Shilpi Goyal's anthology feels like a breath of fresh air.

It should be of interest to both young and old everywhere and successfully travel far and wide!

—**Dr Kusum Pant Joshi**
Writer and Historian

Preface

This wandering heart is on a particular journey to nowhere. Wishing to explore the turns and bends everywhere, sometimes it beats excitedly with a childlike curiosity to know more and sometimes it dives into your own dark depths and discovers a pearl instead.

I've always felt empowered by the magic of words, the way some people might feel empowered by travel or thrive in the spotlight. Every time I resort to writing, it feels like I'm painting my canvas with my own thoughts and choices. In writing, I tend to reveal colours that are hidden inside me, I tend to shine a little brighter. Writing lets me experience the beauty that is quietly woven through my ordinary days. The flights of imagination liberate my soul.

I penned down a little of my heart in these, trying to understand the nuances and shades of feelings, both subtle and encompassing. It was a way of loving life a little more and experiencing colour and essence in the little things. Nature, books, people and life are so inspiring and thought-provoking. I write in the memory of those who have gone but their light remains in me. I write about the feelings that are just ebb and flow, a constant dance of sorrow and joy, pain and love.

While writing, I am silently drawn to this place where I lose myself and find myself, where I experience the contradictory, fascinating, imaginative worlds that exist within us. Writing about myself has helped me embark on a journey of self-analysis. It has been most enriching for me to take this road as it gives me the courage to be myself, feel my feelings, expand my awareness and most importantly, love myself in all my damaged glory.

This short collection of poems that I present here was essentially written for my own self. It was not meant to see the light of day. Choosing to bring them in the open was a difficult decision. But now it feels like walking out into the sunshine after a long, cosy siesta in a dimly lit corner. Deciding to publish this book helped me overcome things I never thought I'd get over. It made me realize that the best part of me is still to be written in my own hand.

If at all, I am able to move hearts, stir souls and stimulate minds with my work, I will consider it my honour. If I am able to encourage even one person to come out of their shell and bring to light their beautiful talent, I will consider my job well done.

1

The Healer

Let me bask in a little sunshine
I've just come of age
The little bird trapped inside me
Has finally fled the cage
My friend tells me I'm a different kind of beautiful
This is something I've never been told
The debris that I detested so much
Turns out to be a mine of gold

The stains were always on the mirror
It took time for me to understand
The faults that I saw in me
Were written but in sand
Let me just revel in my own magic
I've come to know myself quite late
I've finally found my calling
I'm an artist born to create
The life that I've lived is my teacher
My journey is my pride
There's nothing that will hold me back
I have nothing more to hide
I've broken the bars of my fears
And I'm trying to clamber that ascent
I've left behind the cares that fretted me
Or the people who sit in judgement

To that one person who believed in me
When I couldn't trust my own heart
I remain a debtor to your unflinching faith
You gave my ending a brilliant start
For all my rough patches and rough notes
That you have so patiently endured
You might not realize its impact
A hurting soul just got cured.

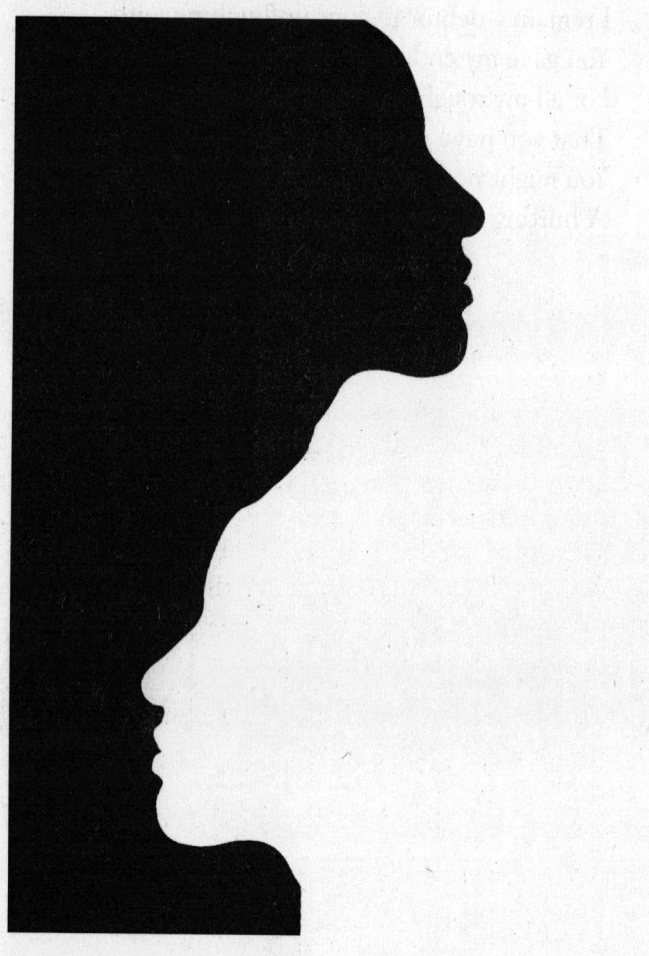

2

I Am Like You

There'll be so much in you
That you'll recognize as your father's traits
The way you hold your glass
And the way you remember the dates
You'll marvel at how your fiery disposition
Has given way to peace of late
And that well sculpted body
Is growing a little overweight

Your father's balding patch
Is peeping from your head
And you eventually speak the words
The essence of what your father said
There'll be a bit of your mom in you too
When you swell with pride at what your children do
And when you smile, those dimples are hers
Also that bout of arthritis, you suffer in winters
You'll be a little like your teachers at school
And a lot more like the friends you made
You'll seek yourself in the books you read
And you'll find yourself in the games you played
All along the journey of your life
There'll be something or someone to claim your being
The subtle nod of your head in agreement

And that stubborn streak in disagreeing

You become a constant reminder
Of things and people from your past
You think you've derailed them
But they catch up really fast
But there's a little voice inside you
That is essentially your own
And when it speaks to you in stillness
Only you can recognize its tone

The wise man that you are
You know it's nothing new
You've carried this lilting voice for ages
And that little light in you
You may not have seen some places
But it gives you a sense of deja vu
And just look at the way you sparkle
In some things that you do

Some out of place memories haunt you at night
And your intuitive mind is always at your heel
You've only arrived here couple of decades ago
But you've lived a hundred years, that's what you feel
You are scared of some unlikely danger
And sometimes your antics surprise your own self
You are but an old soul travelling in a new world
With all old experiences stacked in your shelf.

3

The Storm

At the onset of the storm you rush to the terrace
To bring down your freshly washed sheets
You protectively cover your delicates and whites
Saving them from the slaughter of the sleet

You bolt the banging windows
Lest they should shatter
And you shut the door securely
Against the deafening clatter

You carry your little flower pots to safety
Your pickles and your pets inside the house
Therein you sit with your book and tea
And silently watch the whole world douse

Such is the love for the things you own
A sense of responsibility dawns in a flash
But when it comes to protecting your inner peace
Why do you let your defenses crash

Every time that storm of anger rises inside you
It erodes a chunk of your calm
The sadness that you have housed for so long
Trust me, it is not your soothing balm

That anxiety of the future and regret for the past
It's the wrong bus that you've been boarding
The grudge and faults that you never forgave
They are the gunpowder that you've been hoarding

Release, what no longer serves you
The clutter that you carry, gnaws at your soul
Protect your delicate, white aura
Know your faults and take control

Cement the crevices that are deep
They stealthily let the sorrows seep
Shut out the negativity, dust away the fears
Let the grieving memories wash away with tears

The more you let go, the higher you rise
Your soul is your haven, your own paradise
You carry within you, the wonders that you seek
Let not the storms of the world, ever make you weak.

Magnificent Macabre

What we refer to as beauty, is a vague term
It's a perception, a fixation, it mirrors your mind
That which cannot be contained in a definition
That which we seek, is what we will find

What we refer to as ugly is unacceptance
The monstrosity of things beyond our imagination
There's subdued ugliness in synchronized beauty
And a bit of beauty in deformity and confusion

The diamonds take away the shine and applause
The blackened ashes, hideous, burnt and done
Or is it a beautiful black night just delivering
The first rays of the morning sun

The fallen trees, the swamps and the marsh
The place of stagnant waters and the stench of the herds
It's here that you'll find the treasure trove
The broken feathers of the rarest birds

The carcasses, the blood, the pit and the dung
But the purity of the fire is the same
The dance of the devils with skeletons strung
Is just another misunderstood game

What's pious and what's perverse
Is just a music of broken records
There's sanctity in the tribes of the beasts
Demons too have their sacred Gods

Why must a creature be called beastly
It's born with the survival skill
When it hunts to feed its cubs
There is beauty in that kill
What you reject as horror, blot, ungainly and eyesore
There's beauty in grotesque, waiting for you to explore
Truth is beautiful but so are the lies
We churn a hundred each day, to make us feel nice

Do we really see ourselves in the mirror?
Infinite beauty and ugliness it defies
Does it show the pattern of our thoughts
Behind the bejewelled face and painted eyes

The gurgle of the Ganges and the crescent of the moon
Magnificently adorned by Shiva, the epitome, the best
And the lump of the ugly poison sitting in His throat
Beauty and ugliness, coexisting in who, but the finest

There's beauty in acceptance of ugliness
It's just a phase as in transformation of butterflies
Everything is here for a valid reason
Commit yourself to unearthing the Why's

The Nature remains effortlessly beautiful
Understanding the realm is the only key
Goddess Lakshmi emerged from the same ocean
That in which resided Naag Vasuki

The Gods and Demons belong to the same spectrum
The flower beds or the canopies where darkness is confined
We all carry this speck of the Universe
Beauty and ugliness but a state of mind.

The Space Between

There are two loves you'll experience in a lifetime
Two loves that you'll not be able to defy
One that wants you to live a little longer
The other for which you'll happily die

One love that embraces you in euphoria
Pulls you in its peace and lulls you in a slumber deep
The other that engulfs you in the wonders of insomnia
The distance keeps you up at night, the closeness doesn't let you sleep

One love that brightens your life like a thousand suns
Peps you up, and keeps you soaring high
The other that yearns to hold you in deepest, darkest shadows
If it hugged you, you might just start to cry

One love that marks the strength in you
Makes you humble and thankful in pride
The other that leaves you mushy and dizzy
And let's you unleash that savage side

One for which you'll want the world
Stand like a rock and wipe away the fears

And then there's one which you'll want for yourself
To own its laughter and to cry its tears

One love that holds your hand and leads you to bliss
Or the one that holds your heart and drowns you in abyss
One love that quietens your constant storm in motion
The other that rides with restlessness, like a wave in the ocean

One love where you find yourself
One love where you lose yourself
One love that you deserve like a prize
The other that's your nemesis and your vice

One love is peace and contentment
But one love will burn your soul forever
May you find these contradictory worlds of love
The magnitude of their difference and the wisdom to decipher.

Home

Where are you headed to
Is it a home that you're trying to find
The place of your tryst with truth
The safe house of dreams that you left behind

You'll find your home nestled somewhere
In your mind where the shadows shroud
The haven that takes you in after every storm
That place where you go, to escape the crowd

Your home could be a temple in the corner of the street
Amongst the incense, the bells and the shrine
No matter how many vows you break
You'll come back to the feet of the divine

Your home could be a forest where you wander
Or the beautiful gardens of hibiscus and rose
An indolent moon above the glossy river
It could be a beautiful book or a prose

And if you itch to travel far and wide
Curious, eager, listening to more than what is said
You will find your home in those hidden places
That show up like a road, when you walk ahead

Some will search the whole universe
And build their home in a perfect destination
Others will traverse the path of the soul
And find their home in just one person

They fall in love with a heart full of stars
A longing to embrace them like the sky
The preciousness of being acutely themselves
They get pulled in by a gravity they can't defy

These wanderers, worshippers and silent ones
The lovers of leaving, the gypsy hearts that roam
Someday they'll find what they were missing
In the end, they will always come back home

Home isn't a place where you're born
Nor the earth at the time of decease
It is a place where you have always belonged
Where all your attempts to escape, cease

That book which tells the story of who you are
That niche which holds all the things you love
That place where your spark of life is rekindled
That person who knows you just enough

Home is where the heart is
It's your body that stays in a decorated room
Let your beautiful heart find its home
It will always know where to bloom.

Being Good: The Distortion

Walk a mile into your growing years
Look back at the place where you once stood
The one thing that you'll immediately regret
Is giving up on yourself, trying to be good

You tried to leave a mark on people's lives
Unwittingly, you left a scar on your own
In that fear of people's displeasure
You cut your wings, when you should have flown

You didn't want to do certain things
But you could not bring yourself to refuse
You were upset with people taking decisions for you
But you never had the courage to voice your views

In this process of being good to others
You shrunk yourself for souls who couldn't understand
You learnt the art of existing as a stranger
Into this journey of yours, that others had planned

You were the dreamer, the soft one
The one who saw the world in a grain of sand
You let your goodness get the better of you
It stranded you in an unknown land

You've silently let your life go by
Your magical dance still inside you
Your ache is restless, your echoes are endless
You live a life, wrecked and torn in two

The fear of standing alone
Was in sort, your freedom in disguise
Destiny is simply the strength of your desires
That tag of 'being good' was too much a price

You weren't put on this planet to please
Your mindset is your biggest asset
Never give up on something you really want
It's difficult to displease but it's more difficult to regret

Your dreams are too valuable
To not be lived in every part
You will always own your starry sky
The universe falls in love with a stubborn heart

Must you show your concern for people who matter
Accept whatever their destinies might bring
Wrap them up in your love and poems
But never tie them with your judgemental strings.

Pause

There's no escaping from the voices of the heart
No place quiet enough, where you don't hear your own mind
No matter how far you've made it in life
Those things catch up, the ones that you left behind

Some fears that left you apprehensive
Some ridicule that left you shy
Some criticism and hostility that stunted your growth
Some guilt and shame that never let you fly

The things of the past, if you thought, never last
It's time you think again
It's better to stop running and hiding
It's time you faced your own pain

No one is coming to rescue you
From your low confidence and self-condemnation
Every bit of you is your own responsibility
You are answerable for your own creation

Pause, to let the tears fall
To realize your insignificance and absorb the setback
Pause, to break the patterns that don't serve you
And to mend for once, every weeping crack

Pause, to reacquaint yourself with your pulsing heart
To understand if it's a song, a question or an answer
Pause, to analyse the strength you've built up
You think you are a weakling, maybe, you are a chancer

Pause is that eloquent silence that deciphers
The deepest wounds, the hardest trials
The difference between bond and bondage
The stark truth of unending denials

Pause, to know the difference between
What went wrong and who was wrong
Pause, to withdraw from the ones who fret you
And to recognize the ones who sing your song

You've been running constantly from your inner demons
All this while you've been pathetically alone
There were new love and new friendships that bypassed you
Should you have paused, you would have known

The pause brings along a subtle touch of new hope
Some breathtaking moments that your heart secretly desires
Pause, to see the new little flowers that still bloom
The defiant survivors of your raging fires

There's so much more across the fence
Since when did you lose the nerve to jump upon
There's so much more to that book on your lap
Than the page you are religiously stuck on

Too many people go through life
Without pausing to enjoy what they own
Pause, to reflect upon the life you've made
Pause, to be grateful for every star that shone

No matter how old you get
No matter what phase of life you're going through
May you always pause to fill your pockets with the seashells
Every time the waves bring them for you.

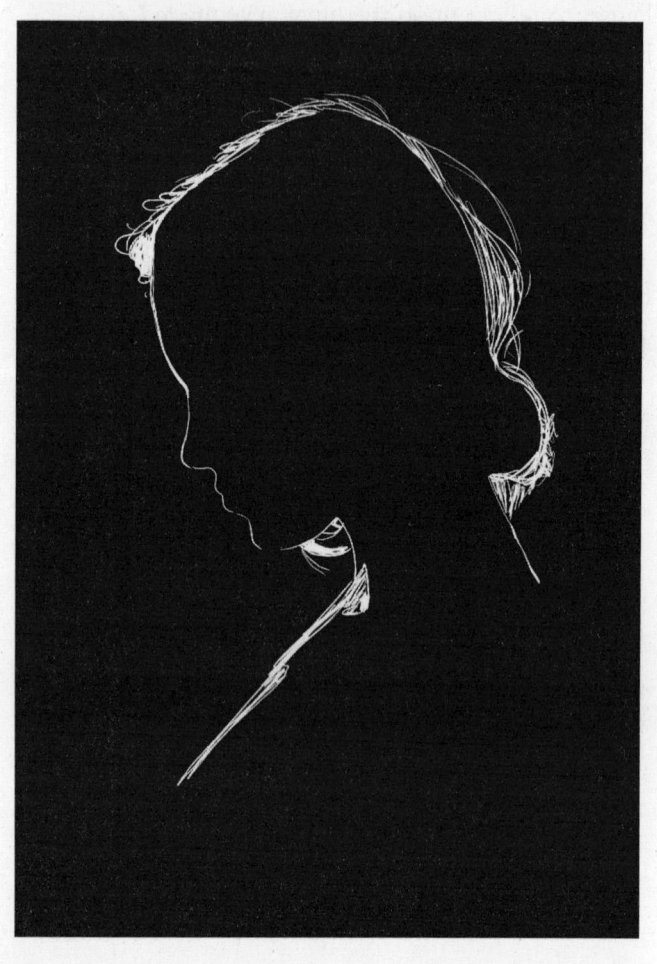

Lost Souls

Success is a beautiful bird
Mostly flying high
And we are all but predators
Aiming for the sky

The purpose of this life is
To succeed, conquer and progress
But there are some like me
Who just love to live, nevertheless

These are the wanderers
The misfits in the room
The ones who'll stop by
And watch a flower bloom

The odd ones who stay to sing
Every time the bells chime
Life passes them by
But they remain suspended in time

These loners, the ones like me
There will never be a record of their existence
But the roads they walk upon
Have deeply felt their presence

The world is a lover
Of the resplendent flowering trees
Yet, the path is imbued with
The grace of their fallen leaves

Who doesn't want to shine
Like the magnificent, splendid sun
Worthy, bright, brilliant,
The blessed and chosen, one in a million

But there are dreamers too
Who gaze at every ordinary star
They are the ones like me
A little broken and bizarre

When everyone is seeking
New avenues to explore
These lovers of self
Sink inside and shut the door

The trailblazers sweep the storms
And deftly set their sail
But some dying embers like me
Softly glow in their mission to fail

These are the givers
The lesser known
The ones who aren't scared of losing
What they never really own

These joyous ignoramus never know
Their power and the worth of their penny
They live in the secret supreme knowledge
They're born to fulfil someone else's destiny

While the world lives on
To capture success and strive
These lost souls like me
Just wish to taste and embrace life.

10

Loner

Have you ever been in those places
Encapsulated among a hundred familiar faces
Laughter, merrymaking and conversations all around you
Yet, loneliness creeps into the empty spaces

It's not that you are a loner
And it's not that you don't indulge in fun
But the things your mind churns constantly
That dish is not palatable to everyone

You delve more on your subconscious mind
And the people out there are slaves to their senses
You give energy to your imagination and your dreams
But the world where you live is barred with fences
You are so awakened to the essence of your soul
The loud crowd doesn't pull you anymore
You realize you have to celebrate your own journey
Your vibe and your tribe waiting for you to explore

You listen deeply to the silence within
It has so much to say to you
Every other voice seems like noise
This conflict is understandable only to a few

You are in conversation with friends
But there's always a book open in your mind
There are questions that you cannot put in words
There are answers you wish to find

Loneliness does not come, from having no people around you
But from being unable to communicate, the thoughts that hound you
When you have taken yourself out of a familiar world
You become a loner even when people surround you.

11

Young Love

The ways you've grown, and the things you've known
Makes you an adult in surety
Let's see what all you've carried along
On your way to maturity

You've carried the stillness of the mountains
And the quiet of the woods deep and dense
Among all the stillness that you've brought along
There's a pounding heart that betrays the silence

You carried the legacy of your family
Their genes in your bones make you wise
Yet you brought along a silent tear
A dew of childhood in your eyes

You've carried responsibility on your shoulders
And you've carried your dignity like a prize
You also carried that tingling love
The one that gave you butterflies

You've carried hope and faith
And the truths you won't deny
That first fling was a forever thing
You've carried with you that little lie

You've carried your boat over the tides
Manoeuvring through the ocean's angry pace
You've carried the ropes to hold your family
Securely tying the knots in place

You also carried some salty water
Gurgling deep in your lung
That memory of the sea on your mind
And the taste still lingers on your tongue

However mature you might become
You carry in you a little wonder and wilderness
A quiet relief and a tremendous belief
In the end, only love can mend your brokenness

For all the beauty that you carry within
Let not anyone call them scars
You are built of strength and wisdom
You're also built of falling stars

Whatever brought you happiness is yours to keep
Maybe it's as foolish as young love of yesteryears
Carry it like a secret, live it in private
It's a fervid flame, forever flickering and fierce.

Travel Diary

Everywhere that I travel
Every corner that I turn
There is a new road awaiting me
A new chapter for me to learn

The winds speak differently
Their sounds tickling my senses
I listen to their howling symphony
Their stories carried across the fences

The arch of the rainbow looms ahead
A painted miracle on the skyline
What could be more colorful and radiant
Than God's amazing creation and design

I marvel at the foam of clouds
Conjuring every image in the imagination's eye
Crowned kings with flowing robes
A chariot with reindeer and whales that fly

The rippling waves and the smooth pebbles
Little prose of love tantalizing my mind
I take in every bit of this magnificence
And release every sorrow I had confined

This wondrous enveloping charisma
This sequined starlit earth
I learn to value my own existence
More than I have sold my worth

I learn to dance more with joy
Than the dramas that spin my life
And I learn to fall asleep peacefully worn out
Than the exhaustion of a worthless strife

I learn to find myself in fulfilment that is mine
Rather than the riches that fade away
An inexhaustible bank of memories
Which I relive day after day.

The Essence of a Woman

When God created woman
He made her a container of grace
She was a special species
Never meant to be in this race

She may not earn a living
But she spends herself every moment, every bit
She is the happiness of her home
She is the vibration, the energy, and she is the fragrance in it

Her kindness has a way of reaching down
Into a torn and weary heart
She may not lift heavy weights
But the way she'll lift up the spirits, that is a work of art

Her gentleness and tenderness
Is her strength in disguise
She's made of earth and stars
She only needs to realize

In her stillness, she understands things differently
In her forgiveness, she learns to grow
She is an epitome of abundance
Endless possibilities and potential in store

She subdues her voice to breathe life into a relationship
Behind her surrender, there's a set of steely nerves
She carries hope in her heart, like a child in her womb
There's infinite love that she truly deserves

There are things a woman needs to do
Remaining in the role of womanhood
She needs to know she's incomparable
Far more superior, far too good
To try to be like a man
She has to step down the ladder
When you do not know your own worth
There's nothing that can be sadder

To every woman out there
Understand that you are beyond comprehension
Your reality is a mirror of your perception
The moon doesn't beg for attention

Take pride in the softness you own
It's a blessing bestowed upon a few
If softness were a weakness
Gardens wouldn't have bloomed anew

So, dump the need to be equal
To walk shoulder to shoulder in this mad race
Your journey cannot be measured by your dainty footsteps
You are much more than your pretty face.

Confused

The books that I read are a different genre
'Heartfulness', 'Soul Consciousness' and an 'Elevated Mind'
The poems I pen are articulate
Apt, comprehensive and well defined

You'll assume I'm some sort of an enigma
Soulful and mindful, mature and refined
Yet if you know me, you will be aware
I am that weird, 'one of a kind'

I'll sit with you and explain at length
Why you shouldn't treat life as a race
But that moment your car overtakes mine
Beware! I will give you a massive chase

I can eloquently express all pointers
Why you should never sit in judgement
But just like that, at the drop of a hat
I can giggle and gossip, resent and lament

I'll read out to you, that chapter on forgiveness
I'll give you invaluable tips on how to let go
Search me and you'll find everything I've held on to
A repository of damage, burning me slow

I can extol the quiet pathways of the mountains
You can picture me, peacefully reading by the logs
Look again and you won't find me there
I've run away, chasing with the dogs

The depth of my soul has learnt for sure
God's love for me is ever so much
The shallows of my heart and mind
Still yearn for a loving touch

The wisdom of equanimity seeps in
Look at life beyond loss and gain
But the eccentric writer that I am
I need to feel every pleasure and every pain

I'll help you learn the techniques of meditation
Your heart, mind and soul, I'll teach you to align
But I have fifteen tabs open inside my head
And music playing from a forgotten time

I know all the powerful words
Bold, independent, decisive and clear
But I'll cling on to your little finger
Acting like a scared child just to keep you here

I know all the therapeutic effects
Of deep conversations with old friends
What I won't give away is my solitude
And the secret of how my solitude mends

It's the truth and it's something I'll make you believe
Blessing of the almighty is all you need
I hope you don't inspect me too closely
I've stealthily covered the traces of my greed

I'll motivate you to do better
Perfection is what you must find
Prod me a little and you will know
How comfortable I am lagging behind

The life that I am living is not truly mine
My soul walks huddled a little behind me
I have made sure I stay hidden and aloof
Surreptitiously hoping someone to find me

What a chaotic place my mind is
Always on the run, forever on fire
I can't be calm and wait on the surface
I'll dive straight in and retrieve what I desire

Not everything about me is growth and maturity
I'm ready to settle for anything that is less
But God understands that I'm still not ready
I still cannot give up my human-ness.

Art

If a painter or a poet falls in love with you
You are sure to live on forever
You'll be frozen in time, preserved in rhyme
Your radiance and glow emanating, like a glistening river

The stars that he scatters on his canvas
Are the trail of kisses he left on your back
And when he writes of the sunlight dancing with the shadows
His mind is visiting you in flashback

His brushes are dipped in finesse to create you
Every curve, every arch and swell
And his words inked in passion
Revealing secrets lovers won't tell

He mixes colours and textures expertly
And the night on his canvas comes alive
And he graces you with a prose that only a lover knows
A brilliant calligraphy from his archive

He is addicted to your dark eyes
It shows in every cloud and each silhouette
And the splash of colours that seem abstract
Are just the dabs of his moments of truth

When he writes of tumbling waterfalls and quiet woods
The flowers beautiful and fields aromatic
He's reliving the moments spent in your embrace
Your splendid charisma that left him ecstatic

He stills you in his art
And possessively holds you there
He draws you out from the hiding places
With a practiced flair

He pens you steeped in magic
You dwell inside his chest
In your beauty he writes poems
In you he finds his best

The painter loves you more in every stroke
Than anyone could in a lifetime
And the poet caresses you with every prose
Your body awakening to the bells that chime

If a painter or a poet falls in love with you
Revel in their light, and stay put therein
They are the ones who know you deeply
And the universe that is contained in your skin.

Shilpi Goyal

Reminiscence

Life is mostly froth and bubble
And we are here to ride along the flow
It's a short and sweet journey
There's no such thing as 'a long time ago'

The memories that seem distant
Are the ones we don't want to think about
And those that really matter
We just have to reminisce and reach out

Memories so palpable as dew
So alive, so fresh as new
The familiar fragrance remains intact
Just a little vision to see that view

We'll find memories propped up in the cushions
And we'll find them tucked in the bed
Some will be displayed on the photo booth
The others peeping through the window instead

There'll be some, found in the disarray of clothes
Some others sitting on that old chair
And most of the times you'll find them in the old songs
And the music that floats in the air

Moments that are burnt into our hearts and mind
Stay beneath all that noise and buzz
And the people who left but never left
They will always wander along with us

It's not the time that heals a broken heart
But it's the choice of the memories we want to hold
Reminiscing a life of laughter and love
Goes way beyond reminiscing hurt written in gold

Get nostalgic about moments that brought you magic
And let the hurtful ones out of your clutch
There's no such thing as 'a long time ago'
Memories linger close to your touch.

Draupadi

A saga of fury and vengeance that reigned supreme
A tale of suffering and disgrace in its extreme
The devilish dance of debauchery and phantom of evils unseen
And yet, life moving from one dimension to another, like a stream

She won't fit into a box, she doesn't remain confined
In the expectations of the world
She gives back what she receives
Every bit of love and or every abuse ever hurled

She's a rebel and she's a dreamer
She's the queen of hearts, starry-eyed, yet earthy
She is the mesmerizing, magical, indomitable Draupadi
A legend, a warrior, a woman wild and truly worthy

Call her Krishnaa, Panchali, Yajnaseni
Born from the fire of wilful revenge
Formidable, yet an epitome of femininity
She is the heroine, the vamp, the goddess, the wench

Shrouded in the filth of blood and massacre
She is a picture of grace and elegance
Enigmatic, with a will of substance
Attack is her only defence

A dream *swayamvar* to the king of her heart
Arjuna, the unparalleled, whom none could outsmart
But destiny had other plans for her
A turbulent journey, right from the start

Won like a lottery, shared like a prize
Draupadi bore the disgrace of being a trophy to five
The sons who could not go back on their mother's ignorant words
Went ahead berserk, and lost her to a game of dice

Pledged like a chattel, dragged like a cattle
Draupadi was brought to the assembly floor
The mighty queen of the bravest men
Oh! What humiliation she bore

To all the wise and worthy men out there
She pleaded and cried till her eyes were sore
She questioned the morality of the humbled sages
She ripped their prestige with abhor

She berated her husbands and perpetrators alike
She tore through their fragmented egos and dislike
She stood her ground and battled with a dying hope
She clung to her faith in humanity like a rope

Dhritarashtra envisions her broken and bare
Through his dead eyes
Bhishma hangs his head in shame
His heart silently cries

Karna burns with hatred
Rejection filled him with despise
Dronacharya dies a thousand deaths
Before his final demise

The lustful lewd Duryodhana
The vile and wicked Dushasana
The progeny of an unworthy king
The worst of the hundred sons

The veil of modesty lay tarnished
In the outstretched hands of the evil player
Krishna O Krishna, wept Draupadi
His holy name in silent prayer

Krishna is the mentor, the friend
Krishna is the God of this globe
Krishna securely covers his *sakhi*
Saving her from disrobe

The seeds of the devastating war were sown here
The bugle of the battle blew loud and clear
Every time a woman is put on the pedestal of disgrace
Be assured, another Kurukshetra is giving a close chase

The world knew not, the bruise that burned the visceral gashes
She rose like a phoenix and burnt her enemies to ashes
Hell hath no fury, like the fury of a woman spurned
She stood defiantly while the world crumbled and burned

The echoes of disaster were replete
The savagery was brutal and complete
No joy, no pride, no sense of victory
That, which was left was an indelible history

Draupadi, the divine, the fiery ember
A fragment enough to burn and dismember
Draupadi, a lesson to be learnt by every human
The deadliest sting is the wrath of a woman

Draupadi, the one who won and lost
Her raging fires untamed by cold frost
Draupadi, the dark indomitable spirit
The ocean of love and the poison in it.

Taken for Granted

There'll be so many instances that you'll remember
The ones that left you confused
The times you went beyond to help someone
And their lack of gratitude made you feel used

Everywhere you look around
You'll find the things that you've taken for granted
Things that you've used to your heart's content
Without which you would have been stranded

The foothold of the rocks
That helped you climb the steep wall
The cluster of the dry leaves
That cushioned your tragic fall

The raindrops, the cool breeze
And the sunlight, if you please
And when your tired bones revolted
That leisure beneath the ancient trees

Whoever stopped performing their jobs
Because you didn't show your gratitude
They are way beyond your ingrate self
Unrivalled in their magnitude

Look back and you'll see
The pinnacle you've held in glory
But that rusted ladder that you used
Never featured in your story

You sang of the wonders of the ship
The beauty that you witnessed on the cruise
You forgot those lifeboats that travelled along
For that moment which you might use

You applauded your grit
The power to cross the dark night
The little lamps on the street shine on
Someone else, too needs their light

These ladders, lifeboats and lamps
Never grudge your thanklessness
They go on to support yet another
Building stories of their success

Every time the world tells you
That you've been taken for granted
Know that you've won, it's a job well done
A new seed of love has just been planted

Next time when someone takes you for granted
Understand that's the highest compliment for you
You are that ladder, lifeboat and lamp
The sturdy one, the dependable few

Submit to love without thinking
Help someone's soul heal
'Thank you' is just another word
Don't let it kill your zeal.

Resonance

How earnestly we seek those who fan our flames
The ones who tune in to the frequency of our mind
Those who fall in step with our weird dance
This resonance, that leaves every noise behind

If you found that sounding board for your emotions
That dreamcatcher where the vibes resonate
You've found the broken piece of your jigsaw
God handpicked this one for your mate

The thoughts that traverse your mind and heart
Their shadows visible in the deep of your eyes
And when you catch that look somewhere
This magical resonance takes you by surprise

You could find it in an abstract artwork or a forgotten song
A dilapidated structure which once stood strong
A fog covered mountain, a dog in pain
A place out of nowhere, but a feeling that you belong

Some phrases of a poem floating by
Some words written for you that leave you aching
The magnetic pull you talk about all the time
It's the thread of resonance, and the fear of breaking

If ever you find your resonating heart
A place, a person, a poem or a song
The thing that you found in flashes across time
Don't analyse, just celebrate and sing along

These moments, places and people are yours to keep
Forever resounding joy in your heart's little deep
Keep searching for those eyes in the crowds passing by
Till you find that spark of infinite, that rock in the steep

Nothing can beat a love that evokes a feeling of knowing
And there's no comparison to that heart that can sense
May your fluttering dreams find their home
Into that brilliant mind that understands resonance.

Dusk

You streamlined your focus to reach
That pinnacle, that coveted stage
And the dreams that got ruined along
Well, that's collateral damage

What you sought for, what you fought for
Will be yours to hold in glory
What lay dead in your fitful tread
Well, that's another story

Little pastures and pretty meadows
Were somehow lost on you
You were vying for the starlight in the night
You missed the tiny firefly that glittered as it flew

Those jubilations and triumphs ruled your head
Those achievements captured in your heart
But the lazy Sundays with friends and family
Their memories relegated to a tiny part

For a long time in your life, you basked
In the warm sunshine of abundance
You rarely thought of the things bygone
Or the people who made you happy once

Perfection was always your thing
Flawless was what you preferred
But all the beauty lay in moments
That were imperfect and weird

And now when the lamps of life begin to dim
The surge of successes don't overflow the brim
Your energies running low and your body won't take charge
And your constant friend is your shadow looming large

In this dusk, the thought dawns upon you
There was so much of magic you missed in lieu
All your life you were so caught up in the chase
But darling you never realized, life isn't a race

Now your mind constantly goes back
To those tiny ordinary details
The picnics under the apple trees
And your furry friends with paws and tails

Those board games and cricket matches
With your insane brood of friends
The whistles, the catcalls, the laughter
The sounds of those moments travel till the end

Your trophies and medals, your fiery speeches from pedestals
All framed for the world to see your prime
But what you lust for are the memories behind the door
Gathering dust and lost in time

Shilpi Goyal

For all the money that you can spend
You cannot pay for what it cost
You cannot bring that resplendent youth
You cannot buy back the moments you lost

You are rich in the love you give away
And you are rich in the friends you keep
Your happiness is the one who stays by your side
When the roads are uneven and the treks are steep

Life is truly a collection of happy moments
Wafting around like your favourite musk
Moments to pick and choose and relive
When your journey takes you from dawn to dusk.

More or Less

Just one more minute of sleep; after that alarm goes off
And just one more hug while the world continues to scoff
Coffee with a little more sugar, an extra scoop of ice cream
And life feels blissfully sated, fulfilled like a dream

A little more of courage, when the night seems darkest
To break free from fear, to make you an artist
A little more acceptance, brings peace and compassion
A little more of love, transcends into passion

A little more imagination, defies the stringent logic
And you live a little more, when you embrace your magic
A little more solitude, to understand the universe
A little shift in perspective, to heal and to nurse

A little more stillness, to find your answers
And just a little more weird, for better or for worse
Just a little more of gratitude for poems and birdsong
And a little more patience when you are not so strong

Wake up a little more to who you are and what's in you
Do a little more of that which sparks a light in you
Be more of a man, you are blessed by the divine
And being a little imperfect is perfectly fine

A good life is a direction and not a destination
Just a little more change, and see your transformation
Trust a little more, the miracles that you see
The world is as you believe it to be

Believe a little more in your amazing uniqueness
You'll always be more, you can never be less.

Perfectly Fine

I'll be a little imperfect and that should be perfectly fine
People around me are maddening, but that shouldn't make me whine
I had no right to the cards I wasn't dealt
But I'm going to play the ones I have, with elegance and shine
I'm the magic that sees beauty everywhere
What I already have, is priceless and divine

I have this one life, one chance to make it count
Just one opportunity everyday, to lie low or surmount
Every vibration within me is a child waiting to be raised
Worry is always an option, but courage is the thing I want on my account

I'll live a little more to experience, than to regret and be sorry
To hell with happy endings, I'm here for the story
I won't look back with my current maturity, at old decisions gone haywire or entirely wrong
They too were a part of my growth, my journey, and my song

I'll idolize the ones who have lost and still learn to dance
The ones who overcame and recovered, where I never saw a chance
The will to stomach all that's confusing, unfair and painful
And nourish my soul each day with an unfulfilled dream or romance

When has life travelled on the path you have chosen
What you thought was evergreen and alive, turns out to be dust, broken or frozen
And when you still live it, love it, and keep creating a new emotion
That's when your magnificent human aspect is rightly proven.

Conviction

I've seen birds who are scared to fly out of an open cage
And elephants, imprisoned by a tiny string of bondage
I've seen insects, who cannot cross the line in chalk
And sprinters, who are now afraid to walk

Yet, I've seen castles that are made out of sand
People who believe their destiny is engraved in the palm of their hand
A torn, beleaguered city, built back like a dream
And the barren mountain, giving way to an incessant stream

You are, what you train your mind to perceive
You are the thunder, the hurricane, you just need to believe
You are that intense energy, wrapped up in a cotton ball
The boulder that you see ahead, is just a mythical wall

You need to step over those fears and tears
The coal turns into a diamond in a thousand years
Let not the fear of height determine your flight
Broken mirrors create the most beautiful pattern of light

Every loss, each setback, treat them with condescension
A mind that is stretched by new experiences can never go back to its old dimensions.

Grief

Grief is an ongoing emotion of the heart
Silently traversing through its niches and bends
You may distract yourself for a while with little joys
But your grief never truly ends

Some days, it will be soft on your soul
Gently flowing underneath your skin
And some days, it will be a cascading fall
Drowning every noise outside and within

Your grief will last as long as your love does
And you know it can be forever
It takes courage to rise above your turbulence
But that path is taken almost never

Grief is a deep longing of the deepest love
The heavy fog keeps returning nights after days
The fact that someone was once there
Their absence continuously stings and stays

When you lose the one you love
A little of you silently dies too
A piece of you goes along with them
And a piece of them, subtly remains in you

To mend your heart, you need to analyse
The role you are playing in your own sufferings
You need a chance to build your broken self
And open yourself to the healing that nature brings

You can smile because they once lived
Or choose to shed tears because they've gone
You can regret and lament their departure
Or cherish their memories and let them live on

You can open your eyes to find them everywhere
In all the wonderful things they have left for you
The sunshine in your smile, the goodness in your heart
Everything that you carry within are their virtue

When a loved one becomes a memory
That memory becomes a treasure to keep
Let yourself absorb the happiness it brings
Let go of the pain running deep

In time, you will know, why people go
In time you'll understand, where they belong
And though this grief stays throughout your days
You'll learn to love and live along.

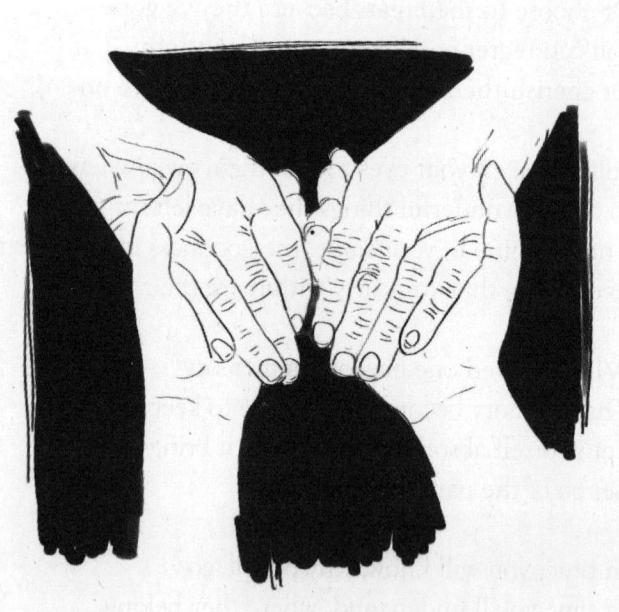

Hourglass

Her mind cannot keep track of time and dates
Of late she forgets many birthdays and anniversaries
And though all important things are locked up safely
She cannot remember where she kept the keys

The familiar faces are easy to recall
But the names tend to confuse her
And if someday she called out to you differently
I hope to God you'll excuse her

The books that she has read over the years
In her memory, those plots get intertwined
Some titles and authors still ring a bell
But it's all jumbled up in her mind

She keeps searching with futility
Her glasses propped on her head
But she never forgets to bow with gratitude
Every time she goes to bed

She can't remember what she had for breakfast some days
At those times she looks oddly tiny and frail
But when she talks of an era bygone
She's aware of the minutest detail

Sometimes she fumbles for a word
An ordinary one that we use everyday
It breaks my heart to see her struggle
When all her life, these words have been her play

Mostly she dwells in her past
Her fondest memories are scattered there
You can almost see her pruning her plants
A little red rose tucked in her hair

She deftly recognizes the singers of yesteryears
The lyrics of the songs on her fingertips
In that moment she sparkles with joy
Cruising ships on nostalgic trips

The lines on her weathered face
Speak of wisdom, triumphs, sufferings and trials
Her breathless, weary, tired body though
A harsh reality to unending denials

She kisses me fondly on my forehead
She wonders how I grew up so fast
She keeps flipping through the old albums
Revisiting the memories that won't last

Everyday she looks at me with awe
When I come back after a hard day's work
And I silently cringe at her ordeal
Seeing her diseased demons lurk

Shilpi Goyal

I still remember that woman of substance
Her confidence and composure topped the list
And the way she always guided me along
Her fingers wrapped around my tiny wrist

Her dreams for me are shiny and clear
Though her vision is glazed and blurred
Though she misses out on other emotions
Her maternal instincts remain undeterred

It's so hard for my paining heart
To lose her slowly, bit by bit
This one woman who stood up for me
How can I ever see her quit

If life ever brings you to a point
Where you have to mother your mom or dad
The only things you'll need are patience and love
And a heart big enough to engulf all that is sad

All they need is your attention and time
They are reeling from the knockouts that life has hurled
They perched the world on their shoulders for you
Now, you have become their entire world.

To Where It Belongs

You've witnessed myriad colours strewn in your path
Whilst walking through the gardens of delight
The flowers blossoming in your rapt admiration
The grass greener for you and the sun a little more bright

But what caught your eye, was a rose wilted and dry
Breezily blooming to the beat of its heart
Too insignificant to be seen, too ordinary to be keen
Not even spectacular to set it apart

You get intoxicated with its perfume
And its lilting songs wafting in the air
For a moment, you thought the songs were for you
And for a moment, you saw that misty despair

Yet the rose sways with grace
Not a drop of your compassion it needs
It dwells on the thorn with which it's born
And on the savage stings, it feeds

What you see is a little misery
Your tender heart feels a trifle sore
But this fragility belies, what doesn't meet your eyes
Is the immense pride it holds in its core

Though the petals may be withered and wane
And the pallor of the leaves gone long
It's the scent of the rose that travel like a prose
And it's the roots that are deep and strong

The rose doesn't get enough sun
You can tell from the shadows that don't form
And its scattered and pebbled bed
Shows it has weathered many a storm
Your pitiful heart aches for the rose
You want to protect it fiercely like a man
You wish to carry it to a place of attention
And give it all you can

You can feel the constant struggle of the rose
And you feel it will succumb to the strife
But what may seem to be its nemesis
Might truly be giving it life

The soil that holds it and the air that enfolds it
They'll never let their sweetheart die
To this corner of the glamorous garden
The rose will live on with a sigh

Wherever in the garden you will be
You'll catch the fragrance of its prose
It needs to bloom where it's planted
Shattered it might be, but forever it's a rose.

27

Maa

The list of your benevolence is long
And my words are jumbled and few
What could I possibly say to express
My ocean of gratitude towards you

The way you lift others up and spread some extra love
You do this when I know you are struggling too
If I call you a rock, a shoulder to lean on, a soothing balm
Every word of it will be so true

All that really matters to you
Is the well-being of the people in your life
This goodness of your heart is your most treasured virtue
You are an encourager and inspirer, I remain in awe of you

You are a vision of silent strength
Hope and love is what you brew
Sometimes you hide your tears behind that smile
And sometimes you've hidden yourself to reassess and renew

Everyone thinks you are the most sorted person
But there's someone else struggling inside of you
Your little heart too gets scared
Enveloped in the dark with a blurred view

Yet you always show the moon
To help us wade the night through
Your stories have given us a motto
But your silences have deep rooted stories too

The way you seem so content and happy
Though your heart might be breaking in two
This show of strength can only be a mother's forte
Carrying the darkest wound in the brightest hue

There were times when you wanted to weep
And there were times you were deeply hurt, I knew
But the grace in which you held your head high
That grace remains indebted to you

I am but a little stream of the vast ocean that you are
And a little verse of the poetry that is you
My blessings are immense because you are my maa
And my love is abundant though my words are few.

Love Letter

Do you remember that time of your life
When you sat down to write a letter
You checked the smooth flow of your pen on rough sheets
And made sure your handwriting looked a shade better

You might also remember the collection of your letter pads
Some official stationery retrieved stealthily from the desk
   of your dad
Some rosy pinks, some delicate blues
Some cartoon imprints in rainbow hues

Some expensive handmade paper
That you coaxed your mom to purchase
And the look that she gave you
Kept you on your toes for days

Do you remember sitting in your favourite corner
Your mood strategically set to analyse
The spellings, the grammar, the content
In your mind you would silently revise

There could be no goof ups
The inked words vehemently resisted erase
And of course, you never knew back then
There are words like backspace

I wish you could see yourself in that age
When you wrote the name of your sweetheart
That one word on the topmost corner
Made you a poet and a work of art

You poured your feelings and proclaimed your love
You penned the promises you meant to keep
Your heart will hold this moment of truth
Forever in the deep

You grieved in words on being apart
You dropped a silent tear on your sacred letter pad
That blot, that smudge and that mess you made
Carried the message that your words barely had

And do you remember tiptoeing to the garden
To pluck that one perfect red rose
To enclose within the letter of your heart
A token of love for whom you chose

The fragrance of that rose still lingers
In every breath that someone took
That ancient rose still resides
In someone's favourite book

The thousand dreams that you wove
The magic written by your hand
Those dreams lie awake in someone's eyes
Those letters securely tied in a silver band

Those precious letters are someone's treasure
A lifetime of love knitted in thread
A world of memories come dancing alive
Every time a love letter is read

I hope you belong to that era
Where every love story was pure and true
And I hope to God you found the one
Whose letters and roses were meant for you.

Abode

They've heard the songs that I have sung
The lyrics of the *aarti*, and the bells that toll
The humming of my mom when she cooked and cleaned
The walls of my house have heard them all

These walls quietly stored in their vault
My whispered secrets and stories said
They've always known my love for writing
And listened in awe, every poem I've read

They have seen me plan my future
Weighing possibilities, making amends
They've absorbed the constant footfalls
The comings and goings of my friends

They've counted the candles on my cake
Held the balloons and streamers for my delight
Patiently adhered, my posters and timetables
And the lamps of the night

They've borne the marks of my sticky infant palms
The blue elephant and a blob of pink for the sun
They still carry the telltale marks
A reminder of my reckless abandon

They hugged me back when I turned to them
With a tear-stained face
They've stoically taken in my punches
And my curses with grace

They've had my back and saved my fall
They kept monitoring when I was growing tall
I've stared at them endlessly, each time I was in doubt
They caved in to give me solace, whenever I felt the world shut out

These walls exude the fragrance of the dahlias I plucked
And the lingering perfume of the incense sticks
These walls have been my pillars of strength
Though you might see just mortar and bricks

The walls of your house remit your energy
Your positivity and negativity stay trapped in its crevice
Fill your space with laughter and love
And what you'll get back, are blessings and bliss.

My Portable Home

My mind is like an opalescent sky
Illuminated by some vivid colours of neon
There are patches that are dense and dark
And a little gray area where I generally sojourn

There are vaults in my head that are deeply obscure
Often I've lost myself in its meandering trails
Some getaways too, which are intensely familiar
Here I stroll nonchalantly when chaos prevails

There's a door called rebellion that I keep shut
The constant knocking sometimes baffles and confounds
The cadence in that closed space is threatening
And when it goes quiet, the deathly silence hounds

There are few little pockets of grief
Hemmed in the fabric of my mind
Their whispers are subtle, soft and undaunting
Like pristine sands that a wave leaves behind

The narrow dark staircase to the upper ramparts
Lead to an attic where I've dumped the irregularities of my fate
Every time I add a wisp of panic or dismay
It shudders in lieu of the oppressive weight

The most traversed path leads to the classroom of morals
The didactic teachings wrestle with my maverick,
　irrepressible thoughts
Sometimes I come out as a jubilant winner
At other times, wounded in the quest of why's and what's

My favourite place remains at the top
A terrace garden imbued with fragrant dreams
A pond of desires where I swirl and swim
Breaking free from the compromised in-betweens

The half-remembered dreams of one true love
Carried forward into the iridescent dawn
The relentless questions stay harboured
The fugitive answers are 'touch and gone'

For all the inconsistencies and unfinished stories
And for all the instances where the going has been tough
My brave little mind has kept its sanity
This portable home of mine has always chosen love.

Too Much

I am too inveigled by the mirages to thirst for the river
Too engrossed in the stars to fret for the moon or its sliver
I'm too complacent to complain and grudge
And too nascent to sit back and judge

I am too prudent to keep explaining my point of view
And too poised to ever take a dig at you
Too celebrated to let loneliness affect me
Too elevated for the choices to reject me

I am too woke to dwell in dreamy delight
Too illuminated to carry the lanterns of the night
Too rich to barter my vibe, my calm
And too big a heart to be held in your palm

I'm too curious to not care for the end
And damn too damaged to care to mend
I'm too platinum to be gold
And too young at heart to ever be old

I am too independent to hold on to your wrist
Too abstract to stay put in your fist
I'm too handful and too much of fun
For some, I'll always be too much of a woman.

Parched

This deeply thoughtful oceanic soul
That wanderlust, menacing curious mind
Where do you you carry me my itching feet
How far is the solace you plan to find

My toes are dying to dig in the sandy beach
I wish to breathe in the mountain air
My heart is lost in the thick of the forest
I want to be here, there, everywhere

I cannot be contained in just a trickle of the rain
The dewy moon holds me just for a while
By the time the sun warms the cockles of my heart
My senses have galloped away a mile

I see love in the soft, sensuous smiles
I hear love in the booming laughter
I feel love in the quiet and also in the blast
Yet I search for love beyond and after

How can I be content with just a speck
This avalanche of light is all for me
How can only one fragrance be my favourite
When I walk under the perfumed canopy

I want all that this universe has to offer
Call me greedy if you might
I believe in the road trip to the stars
Everything for me is beautiful and bright

I'm gentle, I'm wild, deep and mystical
I'm the thinker, the artist, the poem, the dream
I live in sunsets, galaxies, forests and waterfalls
My mind is an incessant, abundant stream.

That One Person

Sometimes when you go quiet,
In the midst of the chatter that you're on
I'll know that a little desire
Just crept inside and made you forlorn

You silently pushed away that lump in your throat
Before catching up to the hilarious part
And when your eyes shine brighter
I'll know
Your unshed tears just broke your heart

The pauses that you take in the stories you narrate
Those pauses have stories too
I'll know every word of what you never said
The impressions of your silence deeply etched in my view

You write to disguise the truth sometimes
At other times you write to hide yourself
But I'll always know the secrets in your poems
And the mysteries hidden in your bookshelf

You've grown more with damage than your age
It gave you loads of gravitas
We live in deeds and not in years
And that's what makes each one of us

Come to me someday, I'll hold your hand
That's all you are going to need
You speak in silence, I'll listen with my heart
And that's the best conversation indeed

I'll read in your eyes, all the questions that arise
The ones you never spell out
You can be footloose and fancy, terrible and funny
And I'll never hold you in doubt

I'll know when to wipe that mole of a tear
That eclipses your glorious star
And I'll know when to wake you up
If your eyelids hide the sky afar

You need to be loved and chosen
Any time, every time and again
And I'll choose you in a thousand lifetimes
Because my choices will remain the same.

Mirage

Don't read too much into me
My words tend to get lost and blurred
You'll search for me in the crowd of people
But I belong to a different world

Don't assume you know me well enough
There's more to me than meets the eye
I walk on the glittering stardust
Beneath which my ruins lie

Don't think you heard the entire story
You just caught a frequency when you tuned
Don't ask me where and how it hurts
I'm too proud to ever show my wound

Don't shower me with praise or pity
Let not my softness make your heart melt
For all you know, I might be carrying
A dagger under my belt

Don't call after me when I'm gone
There's a lot my heart needs to unlearn
I've burnt the bridges I walked along
There's no way I could return

Don't stop me if I break down and cry
An understanding heart too gets spent
Many a storm and ships it has swallowed
The ocean also needs to vent.

Is Your Wrong, Right?

I wish the salient features of wrong and right
Were held in compartments that were water tight
What's right, remained right at every instance, in every game
And what's wrong, would be held responsible for every shame

But the seepage both ways is slow and steady
Our minds have become a confluence already
Yet we need to attribute some sort of semblance
Some mark to differentiate the stark resemblance

It's alright to be a jester for some time
And it's alright to be a target of someone's mirth
But you are wrong when you prolong this game
Let people put you down and lessen your worth

It's alright to lift others up before you
To help them come back on track
But let not your self-effacing humility
Make them put you on the clearance rack

It's alright to have lived a failed relationship
There was so much in it for you to learn
But you're wrong when you put yourself on fire
For someone who stays to watch you burn

It's alright if you broke down sometimes
It's a healing hurt that everyone suffers
But you will be wrong in breaking yourself
Into bite-sized pieces to serve others

It's alright to trust your people
Mostly they will have a clear intent
But you're wrong when you believe those critics
Who read only your introduction, but not your content

It's alright if you never sparkled in someone's expectations
It's alright not to shine in your entire life span
But you are wrong when you don't take yourself seriously
And end up as a pivot in someone else's plan

You are wrong if you don't forgive yourself
For being a jerk in the past
And you're wrong if you get caught up
Only in the first and in the last

You're wrong when you judge yourself
By your age, your looks or a bad day
And wrong again if you think you can't change tomorrow,
What you think is right today

And then there are those things
That are deemed to be wrong
But somewhere, in your journey
They brought happiness along

There'll be vices and addictions
That ruin you in life
Those little doses of sweet poison
That help you breathe and survive

You can call all the things wrong
That made you feel rejected and jilted
But if being right means being happy
Then the scales get vastly tilted

You will be right in listening to your heart
You'll be right in going where it leads you
That's when you become wrong in someone's story
And that's when the conflict bleeds you

You'll be right in taking chances
To explore that life, to find your fantasy
To wash yourself in the tears of joy
To drown yourself in the abyss of ecstasy

But in the quest of your righteous happiness
There will be some loving hearts you crashed
And you become the wrong one in the eyes of all
You get brutally judged and rudely thrashed

We all broke our rules for someone
And we all broke away from the path that was right
And in this wrong turn, the detour that we took
We lived some stolen moments of pure delight

Your mistakes may have been wrong for the world
And while making them you surely grew
If your mistakes made you what you are today
They no longer remain the wrong in you

It's just right to search for happiness
In the places and moments and the things you do
To find that person your soul aches for
And let this joy consume you

It's just right if you worked relentlessly
To fill colours in your gaping cracks
For all your beautiful artwork and talent
People will only see the blacks

Live a life of privacy
No one needs to know the lyrics of your song
You'll spend a lifetime explaining
But your 'right' will always be their 'wrong'

It takes courage walking your truths
Savour the journey soft and slow
Mourn your losses, rebuild your strength
But never let the people know

Don't give up your desires to suit others
Don't reject yourself on the people's selection
The most important relationship is 'you'
That has to be immaculate and carved to perfection

Your soul might wander to the places
Where it feels most alive
Give yourself that permission to travel
That tremendous reason to survive

Take these trips in silence
Make privacy your power
Right and wrong are just your perceptions
You can fall in love with a weed or a flower.

2050

Generation next, all geared up
Robots, computers, tech everywhere
No waiting queues, no sweaty mall hopping
Gadgets galore to monitor and care

Companionships in artificial pets
Caretakers, teachers, all robotic and competent
A chip in the brain to catch your thought
Telepathy, a thing of past, vibes lying dormant

Virtual travels to experience life in other planets
Artificial intelligence in body, clothes and homes
Electric mobility, driverless cars
Packages picked and delivered by super floating drones

An exciting era awaiting to envelope you
Yet, carefully tread, it's a new start
For you belong to the world that's lost
The memoirs of a human, written in heart

The new childhood is captured in digital diaries
Animated series of Cinderella and Lion King
And the shrill voice of Shin-Chan and Doremon
Drowning the lullabies that mom used to sing

The electric rockers and comforters
Have made sure the child gets its nap
It was somewhere in a different world
These comforters were the mothers' lap

The digital love stories, facetime courtships
LinkedIn profiles is what that counts
No more close friendships to gauge a person
Everything summed up in social media accounts

Nuclear families, complicated status
Declining friendships, advanced apparatus
The feeling of vengeance is greater than love
The power and corruption go hand in glove

No more investments in the feeling of trust
Soul calling seems a lost voice
Mindless poems, pointless lyrics
Too little music, too much noise

High-rise buildings
Not a spot of green for the birds
All legal, financial terms
No more soft, emotional words

It's a give and take world
Everything bought for a price
No place for magnanimity
And none for sacrifice

Live, if you must, this life of extravaganza
But remember that life before this was also nice
Let the good old soul live in you
A body without a soul cannot suffice

You can fill your house with flowers and incense
Aromatic candles, the best that you have smelled
But the perfume of goodness that is in you
That fragrance remains unparalleled

There is magic in believing in yourself
Your confidence oozes and tops
But somewhere in the process of ascertaining your belief
A learning process stops

Live a life in rainbow colours
Explore the irrepressible neon
But remember that grey is also a colour
And life will surely go on

Grow, but carry little moments within you
Memories to sustain in a world so new
Be kind, rather than being one of a kind
Carry strength, hope and a little childhood dew

Enjoy the freedom of being advanced and alone
Rise from the ashes of failures and flaw
Whichever generation you may belong to
You'll always be part of the huge jigsaw.

One-Sided Love

You breathe life into the places you walk in
Unwittingly, you take my breath away
The smooth talker that you are
You leave my heart in knotted disarray

Everyone flocks around you
Who doesn't want angels in their lives
But I'm just an ordinary human
Flustered in my flaws and lies

You raise a little storm in me
Every time I look at you
The world doesn't need to know
Thunders can be silent too

Some fabricated thoughts my mind spins
And believes them to be true
You too love me in the same ferocity
That, in which I love you

Don't just listen to what the lips are saying
There's a story hidden in my eyes
Some questions are too prudent to be asked
They float around you in disguise

The way I seem to be happy around you
That's a talent I have honed
My laughter and my vibrance will deftly hide
My reluctance that I've secretly mourned

You were dumb at dumb charades
Not a thing you ever could guess
My unsaid words stayed with me
I could not bring myself to confess

However hard I wipe away
Some people stick on to the corners of my heart
Stubborn people and stubborn memories
It's impossible to keep them apart

An epic I wrote on you
And an eternity it took
But I don't even feature as a chapter
In the story of your book

Some love stories are written in destiny
And some, written together under the stars
Yet, some are written alone in darkness
Smoldering beneath the wounds without scars

One sided love story, is a mystery in every page
Who's a bigger loser, it is difficult to gauge
The one who loved but could not show
Or the one who missed out because he did not know

Nevertheless, one-sided love
Is beautiful in all that it creates
Some abstract memories to last a life time
And some fantastic stories to narrate!

Solo Trip

The phase that I'm going through
The place that I'm going to
That altitude and destination
Is not meant for everyone

There are baggages of expectations
That I have left behind
And the memories of the past
That I've out run

My reality is my perception
Which has always been a little off beat
I could never be like my friends and family
Or the dreams of the people I meet

I choose to look for niceties everywhere
My state of mind is generally upbeat
The beauty of raindrops envelop my mind
Even though I sometimes slip on the sleet

Often I've been told
To become a little more bold
Not to buy every sad excuse
They are gimmicks to be sold

To not believe in the goodness projected
Those times were gone and old
To think of a plating or polish
Whatever I see as gold

To hold back my emotions
When someone narrates a story
To cork my compassion
If ever I feel sorry

To understand the jibes, the vibes
The things that are not said
To manipulate my conversations
To sharpen my dull head
To give back with the same force
The utter disgust people throw at my face
To let them know I'm no doormat
But a cyclone under my soft grace

My friends, family and well-wishers
Constantly egg me on
To make me brave and wise
A strong bull with a horn

They take the responsibility
Of carrying me along
To the places and mindsets
Where I don't belong

How can I tell them silently
That I have a different heart
This show of bravado and gusto
Simply tears me apart

Beneath this veneer of softness and grace
I have nursed only malleable dough
What you see is just what I am made of
There is not much in me to hide or show

There are times I have known the lies
And seen through the tears
And I've let them lead me on
Because I had my own fears

The misery of witnessing a facade going down
Looking in the eye of the one who got exposed
It's as brutal as being caught in a shame
When perfection is all that you have posed

To accuse and expose what no one knows
It hurts more than being taken for a ride
I'd rather lose a penny and a point
Than to see someone lose his pride

If I could be of help to anyone
Why should I consider myself used
If my knowledge built someone up
How can my intelligence get abused

It's okay if I prop someone up my shoulders
I'm sure they're strong enough not to break
I'll congratulate the one with a better deal
My respect is as firm as my handshake

My journey is entirely mine
And I have to take a solo trip
The people I help on my way
Will also grasp me when I slip

What's wrong in thinking that the earth
Is just so beautiful every morn
Soft people can suffice too
Like roses on a thorn

I'm happy for people's happiness
And I am sad for their misfortune
Who am I to judge if karma beat them up
Why should I sing that under tune

We live in a parallel world,
The soft ones who you think are misfits
Once in a while we come out in reality
To suffer the pangs of these visits

While I move away slowly I feel sorry
For breaking the heart's trust and hope
My friends and family love me deeply
But they don't understand and I can't cope

I'm happy to be where I am
I'm much more human than you think
There are heights that I'm aware of
Even though you're sure that I will sink

Let live the people who love differently
Don't keep telling them they are wrong
They too will live their destiny
They too will swim along

There are people who cure with surgical knives
Some can cure with their knowledge of right and wrong
But there are a few who know how to heal
With their heart and their soulful song.

That Love Story

That love story
Unbound by time
Untouched by promises
Unspoiled by expectations
Unblemished by words
Goes on, sails across, transcends
The turbulence of change
The depravity of leisure
The infinity of distance

That love story
Sunk in the bottomless silence
With innumerable floating words
Unsaid, untold
Wrapped in the blanket of longing
Densely quiet, immensely calm
Yet, a constant desire to unfold

That love story
Thrives on a droplet of faith
Pulsates on the beat of hope
Feeds on the platter of dreams

That love story
Becomes the canopy of your scorching life
That balm, that everlasting calm
It stays alive in your soul
You carry it with you
In every relationship of your life
In every situation or strife

That love story
Your subconscious mind silently keeps
You meet with it
In the deepest stage of your sleep

That love story
Breathes love in you and me
We hold in our hearts, this love for eternity.

See Yourself

Let me walk you down the mesmeric aisle
That maze of the magnificent mirrored hall
Everywhere you look, you'll find yourself
A thousand images in every wall

I wish you see yourself in the perfect light
That vision of yours which has left me flattered
I still keep chasing the dancing butterflies
And the remnants of rainbows that you have scattered

I wish you see yourself when you read a book
Curled up, unmoving, your eyes absorbing the fluid print
Sometimes you sigh and hold on to a line
A memory, a dream, a desire in a teary glint

I wish you see yourself in moments when you sleep
The whispers of your breath silently floating by
There's beauty in the serene and calm composure
Like the moon slowly traversing the inky sky

The nightshirt of mine that you fondly wear
The warmth of love exuding from your skin
I wish you see yourself in moments like these
Each thread of your beauty is intricately woven

You do not know the magic you look
When you are brimming with laughter and chatter
Naughtiness and grace, captured in your childlike face
Your voice, the sound of pitter-patter

I wish you knew how beautiful you are
Gazing at the early morning sunrise
That face, when you want to tell me something
Those eyes are full of wonder and surprise

But most of all, I wish to show you
The way you look when you look at me
A fluttering heart in the deep of your eyes
A tornado rising in the gentle sea

You are the beauty of boundless imaginations
Sensuality, vivid colours, poetry and art
I wish you see when you are truly yourself
So authentically beautiful, you tug at my heart

This love that flashes and flames constantly
Mystical, hidden, yet so palpable and mine
For once I wish, you see my scorching scars
I burn in your beauty that I cannot define.

Acknowledgements

This book is a summation of the unfading love and trust my friends and family have reposed in me. I am indebted to their invaluable assistance and enthusiasm while this book was progressing.

I am thankful to my husband Manish and son Tanishk for their unwavering support, and my dear friends Kamini Sharma and Tanmay Kishore for their consistent encouragement and unfazed confidence in me. Lastly, I am grateful to my mother for always blessing me with her love in all my efforts.

Home is where the heart is,
It's your body that stays
in a decorated room.